Since Bloomsday June 16th, 2022, Historical Society completed a Poe competition titled 'The Writer's Ad _____ as part of their successful two day Bloomsday Festival. In 2024 the prizes were presented by Marie Heaney, the wife of the late Nobel Laureate poet and author Seamus Heaney. When the winning poems had been read out and prizes collected, Marie commented to me that the standard was very high and I had to agree. It was then decided to bring all the poems entered into the competitions to a wider audience and through this endeavour we could raise some finances for a local charity. If you are reading this, you have bought and a copy and thank you for your support. We hope you enjoy the talent emanating from our great community.

The contents herein represent the poetry entries from the Bloomsday Festivals 2022 - 2024

Eddie Bohan

Chairperson

Ringsend & District Historical Society
TELLING A 1000 YEARS OF RINGSEND HISTORY
Dedicated to the memory of Orla Murphy

FORWARD

Earlier this year it gave me great pleasure to accept an invitation from Ringsend & District Historical Society to present certificates to the local writers who participated in the Writers Adventure event as part of the Society's 'Bloomsday Ringsend' project. On June 16th last as I sat in St Patricks CYMS Hall on Irishtown Road and I was captivated and moved as the poems and short stories written by young and old from the locality were read out.

This initiative by Ringsend & District Historical Society to provide a platform for local writers is a testament to the Society's farsightedness and commitment to its community. The stories and poems within this excellent book capture the Community's heartbeat, its joys and sorrows, its memories and wit and its challenges and successes. It makes for a thoroughly enjoyable read and gives a real sense of one of Dublin's oldest Communities.

My late husband Seamus Heaney and I both had a deep sense of community in our many years together here and this book reflects the very essence of community.
I hope you enjoy!!'
Marie Heaney   November 2024

CONTENTS

Re – Joyce by Thomas Gregg

Ringsend by Jennifer Betts

Ferry Ferry by Mary Lou Dent

I'm Ready Hun by Aoife Connolly

The "Black Thing" in the Cockle Lake by John McCann

Here Be Monster by John McCann

I Remember by Karl Pepper

Raytown by Gay Byrne

Before & Never Were you Twenty by Shay Connolly

Christmas By Séanna Connolly Sheridan

Full Circle by Michael Gregg

You Made a Man of Me by Shay Connolly

Ringsend and Me by Gay Byrne

Over The Bridge Into Ringsend by Joe Behan

In Ringsend by Madison Tucker

The Poolbeg Lighthouse by Thomas Gregg

On a Bench by Suann Moore

The Grief Manual by Sophie Gregg

Another September by Eithne Cavanagh

Sunday Morning Walks After Mass by Mick Brady

The Lady Re-Purposer by Eithne Cavanagh

Blessed by Mick Gregg

The RIC by Tim Flood

Alphabet Soup by Thomas Gregg

The Widows' Bakery by Eithne Cavanagh

Growing Up By Anonymous

Anonymous

Today by Eithne Cavanagh

Cure for a Whitlow 1958 by Mary Guckian

Re – Joyce by Thomas Gregg

I am not James Joyce
No that never could be
Yes indeed he had a vision
That very few could see

Great scholar's gather yearly
For debate and conversation
From learned institutions
They travel to our little nation

Still very few find the true meaning
Of the words that Joyce wrote down
Especially his masterful description
Of his beautiful yet different Dublin town

Yes old Dublin affected him deeply
This town his tongue did rightly acclaim
As begrudging church and state hierarchy
Tried to obstruct and deny his truly deserved

literary fame

Who is Joyce they ask

Sure haven't we all got a view

A dirty perverted man back then

Or a genius that no one even knew

Yes, die before your true reward

The applause of those so called peers

Not much use these accolades

After poverty stricken years

History much kinder now

Yes James you are rightly revered

But isn't it the ultimate irony that

Same people cheer who once jeered

A hero on one's doorstep

Much easier just to ridicule

Everyone else is doing it

Better join in and look cool

Wouldn't it be nice to talk to you and say
Yes James you once were the true prodigal son
Denied the opportunity to prosper
Maybe second time round you could be the special one

Oh James we failed you so
Too bitter to let you flourish
It wasn't the thing to do back then
Don't dare nurture or encourage

Look at your final resting place
The church and state had the final say
Buried in a single grave
Quite conveniently far far away

Ulysses your Bible for the people
In its own peculiar way
All you want is for it to be heard
No need to genuflect kneel or pray

Ringsend by Jennifer Betts

On the banks of the Liffey,
an old town does dwell,
where the locals put you under their spell,
with tales of old and generations of many,
where the front doorsteps are as clean as a penny
the buildings stand tall, preserved & untouched,
one reason why it's loved so much, but it's the
people who really make the place
and you'll always find a familiar face, you may get
jibed, for being a blow in,
but guaranteed, you'll have a relation of kin.
Where traditions are steeped in history,
where the community spirit thrives, where there
have been many lives. You'll never forget your
experience, nor find a better friend,
it will touch your very soul, in this town called
Ringsend.

Ferry Ferry by Mary Lou Dent

As I stood on the Jetty,
And stared out to sea,
Knee deep in water,
Wished it was me.

Good morning Paddy, not a bad day,
As onto the Ferry they made their way,
Fifty men on a boat built for ten,
Ah sure that was back then.

We'll have one in O'Connor's first,
This sea air gives us a thirst,
Sandboats, cattle boats and boats from Japan,
Come on Noely, you're in our gang.

Blinded by the soda Ash,
Giant Cranes swing to and fro,
While earning every penny,

As they lift and load.
They'd meet up in the canteen,
Telling tales to beat the band,
Me uncle was delighted,
When Jimmy Steward shook his hand.

Waiting for the whistle to blow,
Along the north wall ,they would go,
With leather patches, on coats of wool,
All standing watching, a lonely Gull.

They see him in the distance, He's coming to Ferry them home,
Down the step go these hard working men,
With caps of grey, and hooks in hand,
Across to Ringsend,

Ah sure that was back then.

I'm Ready Hun by Aoife Connolly

I'm ready hun.
May this be the year
You release all that fear

All this waiting
Self-hating
Contemplating, just
Leads to procrastinating
The mind is so fascinating

Reflecting

Inspecting

Projecting

Rejecting

Yourself,

Leaving your dreams on the shelf

Is it too late?

Do I just wait?

Am I too old?

Leave your dreams in the cold.

Maybe I should just do what I'm told.

Settle down

Party on

Forget your dreams

Stay strong

Expiry date

Find yourself a soul mate?

Lose some weight.

Pound or judgement?

Opinions or begrudgement?

Instagram

Feel like a Sham
Does anybody even give a damn?

Too much thinking
Feel myself sinking

"Turn that frown upside down"
But then I drown.
Then I turn it all around

The show must go on
We must try to get along
Come together in song

Goodbye 2020
You've been plenty
But we've felt empty.

2021
I'm ready hun.

The "Black Thing" in the Cockle Lake by John McCann

As kids in Gilford Avenue we were blessed to live in the armpit of Dublin Bay.
The world was always ok once a few basic things were in place.
At the top of the avenue looking out to sea, we checked from left to right.
The dump was still there, then the power station, then the Wall and the red lighthouse, Howth Head, then the Kish, then Dún Laoghaire and its mountainous backdrop, the broken baths and the tower.

But most of all, the black thing in the Cockle Lake, slightly off to the left and a few kilometres out.
The black thing was a wrecked funnel from a wrecked ship.

It sat upright, buried in the sand at the western end of the lake, a gatepost to the glorious "Cockeller".

It was sunken into a large crater of soft sand and was barnacled, rough and ragged.
It had become a biosphere before biospheres existed and we hunted crabs, flats, hoppers and shrimps in its moat.
We loved the black thing.

Then one morning in the aftermath of a severe sea storm we went up to run our checklist. Dump, chimneys, wall, lighthouse, Kish, mountains, baths, tower…all in place.

But the black thing…WAS GONE.

Well, panic stations. A gallop back to the house to

get everybody and a reassembly on the strand wall confirmed everything.

The black thing was gone.

We assumed it had been washed out to sea, but as we piled over the wall there it was, broken against our own granite sea battlement.

We viewed it like a family member and we were all upset when the corpo truck came to take it away.

We fixed ourselves with a little hike out to the black things crater, to pay our respects.

We loved the black thing.

Here Be Monster by John McCann

Legends lurk in all maritime environments. In the mouth of the Dodder at a right angle to the Liffey and just under Ringsend Bridge, lived the Muck Monster.

On low tide, the Dodder was an open artery of congested muckbanks with a silvery snake of water running through the middle. This wasn't common or garden muck. This was Ringsend muck, thick and gloopy with the strength to suck anybody and anything to its doom. Stark evidence lay just opposite the GRAND CANAL DOCKS sign where a significant wooden vessel had been gripped, never to be freed again. Its planking and decking long gone, the ribs protruded like pleading fingers from the muck looking for a saviour to pull it out.

We were Sea Scouts. We were 4th Port Dodder Sea Scouts, based on the riverbank at Derrynane Gardens just opposite Stella Gardens and at the back of the famous Shelbourne Dog Track Stadium. 4th Port were the best.

Sea scouts were brave and were always prepared and we were afraid of nothing. We forayed up and down our little stretch of river and beyond out into the Liffey, up and down, rowing and paddling a variety of skiffs, punts, canoes, coracles and rafts. On odd occasions, we would follow the trade routes to Dollymount, Islandbridge or Dún Laoghaire, on very important business.

The Muck Monster was silent and almost invisible. Its best chance of getting us was when we were mud-larking in the river looking for rowlocks or other items that that fallen overboard and had sunken into the mire. Our black wellies would squish into the muck and incomprehensible suction would hold us firm and stop us from pulling our legs back out. The Muck Monster thrived on black welly boots.

The other problem with the Muck Monster was that it could manifest itself into a physical being and slurp its way through the cracks in our bedroom windows and turn up at the end of the bed at night, after dark, if you didn't believe in it. We didn't believe in the Muck Monster. We were big boys.

As we marauded our way up and down the rivers and the sea, sunburnt and savage, we feared nothing and nobody. Stone splitting sunshine, relentless rain and wailing winds were the elements of our boyhood. We would face down Blackbeard himself.

At the end of the energy sapping day, on the odyssey home in the dusky evening, the body burned out from labour, the mind would begin to kick in. With salt stained skin and stinking of seawater and seaweed, all the day's snapshots and flashbacks of frantic activity would be collated to make sense of it all.

Then it would happen, as dusk turned to darkness. We remembered. I do believe in the Muck Monster. I do believe in the Muck Monster, I do, I do, I do.

I Remember by Karl Pepper

I remember living in Stella as if it was a past life,
I lived in Stella most of my life.

I remember Tom's where powers now stands
and Cody's cause I was sent by my nan.

Get me a pattern and this wool too, here's 50p
between me and you.

I remember the days up the green we played,
football and toys, those were the days!

All neighbours were known, all kids played out,
home before dark without a doubt.

The area has changed but community lasts, I still
remember.....
My past

Raytown by Gay Byrne

Most summer mornings
We spent playing rounders
Most summer afternoons in the
lake standing on flounders

Our Ma's would say boys
come back home soon
No such thing we'd spend
all day on the lagoon

We'd ramble up to Sandymount
To do things illegal
Get back with our apple's
In time for the Regal

Jump off the jetty steps into the Liffey
Cold and dirty out in a jiffy
Put clothes on that were damp

And laugh at Sandy the tramp.

Coats put down in Ringsend Park
Sides picked we'd play until dark
It was so bad we could not see a sinner
Someone suggested next goal the winner

At times we'd meet and go down
to the dumps
If you got chocolate and crisps
You had come up trump's

Dockers going to North's
Dockers going to Smith's
When the pub's closed
Ferrari's for ray and chips

The lads lay their nets
for a ne'er a one
Salmon going up
The Liffey to spawn

When the bailiffs arrive
The lads are well gone

Boats on the river, race has begun
Down to the hail and back
Cup is collected Paddies have won
it's up to the Yacht for the craic.

Wednesdays and Fridays
Hear the fishmonger sing
Now mam would you like
a backbone or a Wing.

Raytown's different, it's just not the same
No orchards, football, jets,
No rounders, flounders, nets,
No Regal no dump progress to blame.

Before and Never were you Twenty
by Shay Connolly

Who stole your blue and pink baby grow
Before you grew at all
Who discriminated you
from the day that you were born
Who dipped your pockets of the money
that should have been there
As your divvy of the Nation's wealth
And rang it up to their own greasy till
Before and never you were twenty

Who stole your education
Your books and pens and all
Who dried your inkwells
That made your quill illegible
And who stole your equal opportunity
And locked it in their garden sheds
All for themselves,

To mow their lawns when their grass was long.
- Before and never you were twenty.

Who stole your neighbourhood
To build big shiny glass windows
That only saw you in a reflection
Of their own creation of the Sun
And who threw scraps of their left-over lunches
For you to fight over with your best friend
Until you made up again
On a benchmark in Mountjoy
Before and never you were twenty.

Who looked at you as different
Because you said Dart instead of Dort
Inhaled hash, instead of cocaine
Wore runners instead of Hush Puppies
Who sneered at you because of your chewing gum
While they chawed your jawbone
Of its flesh
Until you could speak no more

Before and never you were twenty
And who sliced your birthday cake
And put the jam piece in their briefcase
And left you with the crumbs.
Who stole your cobblestones
And paved them like Sunset Boulevard
That only they could walk
And shoved you to the side streets
On each and every birthday
Before and never you were twenty.

And who allowed your roof and slates
To be picked up by a Vulture
In one big sweeping swoop
And left you naked in the rain
And who stalked your everyday
Until you fell dishevelled and broken
Waving your white hankie
For them to blow their noses with
Before and never you were twenty

And who denied your democracy
When you voted for change
When you saw a new candle burning
Far away from the Church gates
Who then labelled you unworthy
To dine in their Restaurant
In case you would pass your saliva
On to their finest cutlery
Before and never you were twenty.

Who forced you down a laneway
Where they deposit all their waste
Who forced you into an abandoned car
Where you sheltered for the night
Who slowed down your every breath
Along the path of life
Until your last breath quenched out the fire
That had hiddenly enraged all your intestines
Before and never you were twenty.

And when you passed

Who hid you from the airwaves

While they talked and walked

With the new Minister for Housing

And his promise to end it all

Like the promises of a hundred years before

As he flew like an Eagle out of the radio station

To meet the Vulture and build their nests.

Before and never you were twenty.

In memory of a homeless man who died in an old burned out car on Parnell Street, where he was sheltering RIP.

Christmas By Séanna Connolly Sheridan

Christmas is more than a day in December ,
It's a day where we do things we will always remember,

Its drinking hot chocolate on the couch,
All the laughter filling the house,

All the families sending out cards,
Wrapping ourselves in coats and scarves,

Watching movies chilling in bed,
Putting gloves on our hands and hats on our heads,

Christmas is more than a day in December,
It's a day where we do things we will always remember.

Full Circle by Michael Gregg

From the circular carvings on the kerbstones of
(Bru Na Boinne) Newgrange
To the intricate spun stories of life in Dublin
Joyce paints a full circle that life will arrange
With little thought for Opinions and who it is he is
troublin'
To hell with the State and the government, and
that self-serving Church
He stabbed stealthy paint strokes from his own
pulpit's perch
Calling the muses to focus his aim
He filled his pages leaving all to exclaim
He is offensive, he is vulgar
But, is it he who is guilty -who points the finger?
His manifest was Life is Art and Art is living
That piercing eye of his saw it from the beginning,
To fulfil this belief he knew he must fly
Taking Nora away from the home they both adored

Never stopping to think and write about home
until he expired.
His longing and yearning for the real happiness in
life
Was buried deep in the words he did write
Look deep in the heart and you will find the love
that is there
It exists when you were born and
will till you expire
As the moon circles us
As the years spin along
This circle of life
Is our one true song.

You Made a Man of Me by Shay Connolly

Recalling James Joyce's first date in Ringsend with his wife to be Nora Barnacle after she had stood him up previously. That encounter left such a mark on Joyce's life that he chose that day, June 16th, 1904 to be the central date for his now famous world book Ulysses.

Oh, I am a complicated Irishman
That many found me hard to understand
For I spent my young life writing in the dark
'Till I found my true love in Ringsend Park

Oh Nora, Oh Nora, comfort me
You're the only one that ever set me free
Oh Nora, You made a Man of Me

We cuddled in Ringsend and a little bit more
On the 16th day of June, Nineteen hundred and

four

When my saviour turned up to be my Noah's Arc

Oh I'll ne'er forget that day in Ringsend Park

Oh Nora, Oh Nora, comfort me

You're the only one, that ever set me free

Oh Nora, You made a Man of Me

Oh your long and lovely buttoned velvet glove

That you took off to show your independent love

And your saintlike eyes, they shone like a Lark,

Forever we'll remember Ringsend Park

Oh Nora, Oh Nora, comfort me

You're the only one that ever set me free

Oh Nora - You made a Man of Me

Now our Love survived and we grew old together,

We're just like two birds of that auld feather

And your quirky eyes, still ignite the spark

Of that warm and tender day in Ringsend Park

    Oh Nora, Oh Nora, comfort me
You're the only one that ever set me free
    Oh Nora, You made a man of Me
    Oh Nora, You made a man of Me.

Ringsend and Me

An Appreciation by Robbie Cronin (Teacher)

As a teacher who began teaching in Marian College in 1984 and finished teaching there in 2019, Ringsend holds a special place in my heart. 35 very happy years full of cherished memories, many of them being of Ringsend and Raytowners. A place I love and feel part of!

Teaching for me has always been both a social education as much as a field for academic learning. And my many highlights have involved the social sphere, that element where teachers go outside the classroom and engage with their students in other areas. And the old adage that teachers learn more from their students than the other way round is so true for me. I have learnt so much from the proud Raytowners, their pride of place, their loyalty, their togetherness and, most of all, their sense of fun. Their wit and one liners had me bursting my sides laughing on so many occasions! Now, to gain their trust is not easy but, when they trust you , they are tops ! No better bunch of people can be found anywhere else !!

I looked after many football teams throughout my time in Marian College and it was this involvement in sport which allowed me to get to know the people of Ringsend so much better. My dealings with teams have opened doors into the heart of Ringsenders. I have particular fond memories of Sean Gannon who coaxed me back into coaching. Daniel and Dean Kelly who also play at high levels were superb and the likes of Lee Weafer and Wayne Byrne who do so much work for St, Pats CY nowadays were also superb for Marian College. Lots of Ringsenders represented Marian with pride and by so doing brought pride, honour, distinction not only to Marian but to their area and themselves. What an honour it was for me to be involved in their development and their successes!

I remember my first few years, going back as far as 1984, when I had to set up the goals, the nets etc. As a young man I felt somewhat intimidated because I had to deal with the Ranger, organise the boys and ensure nothing went wrong both on and off the pitch. This was all done on my own initially but as the years went by Cambridge Boys came to my assistance came to my assistance more and more. I soon discovered that once the locals trusted you and that my involvement was not just a ticking the box exercise, there would be lots of help available. The likes of Thomas Gregg and Rocky O' Brien who have done so much for football in the area were a huge help to me. Although they will never realise how much they have done for the health and wellbeing of so many adolescents in the area. I hope they, and so many other local coaches know, that Marian would never have won anything were it not for their involvement with their clubs!! Míle buíochas!

The highlight of my many years in Marian was 2013

when the senior soccer team wont a prestigious Leinster competition. The team consisted of Ringsenders like Rocky's son Ian, Ciarán Stafford, Stephen Middleton, Thomas Walsh, Daniel Boulton, Seán O'Connor and Daniel Kelly. Brilliant players who developed more through their local clubs than through Marian! And it's no wonder we achieved so much success that year! I always said that Ringsenders were born with a ball at their feet and had more footballing ability in their small toes than I ever had in both my feet! All the lads had to do was believe in themselves! And when they did and, very importantly, controlled their tempers, the world was their oyster!!

I spent five of my last years in Marian acting as home school community liaison coordinator. This job was difficult enough in that you had to engage with parents who were encountering difficulties. My job was to be there for them, to show them that the school was there for them and their children and no shame, blame or unease should be felt by them. This entailed a high level of trust and fortunately my involvement in sport helped me so much in creating this feeling of trust. Parents were seen talking to me at the side of pitches, knowing so many people in St Patricks Rowing club as well as Stella Maris, my association with Clan na Gael and of course, football, opened so many doors for me! People in difficulty would see me stopping on my bike to have a chat with the late and great Larry Dunne, or with Michael or Liam Bannable, and with the Montgomery's. This showed that the locals trusted me and this visibility made me someone to be trusted. I was almost one of their own !!

Now that I have moved on from Marian College, my connection with Ringsend has not ended. James McMahon and Barry Montgomery invited me to join the Irishtown House golf society. How privileged, proud and happy I was that some of my past pupils saw fit to ask me to join their society!! When I go back to Irishtown House after a game of golf, I invariably meet some parents or students I would have met during my professional career. It is a huge thrill to see how these men have done so well in their lives and to think I had some small part in their development. I feel so grateful!

Ba mhaith liom mo bhuíochas a ghabháil la Shay Connolly agus le lucht eagraithe na Féile seo! Guím gach rath oraibh go léir.
Míle buíochas le muintir na Rinne! I owe you so, so much!
Le meas,
Robbie Cronin

Over The Bridge into Ringsend by Joe Behan

Growing up on South Lotts

Was full of family forget-me-nots.

To visit relatives our parents did send

Us over the Bridge into Ringsend.

From Canon Mooney Gardens to Pembroke Cottages

And on to St. Patrick Villas

If we didn't visit them all

The mother would kill us.

And even when those visits came to an end

We still went over the Bridge into Ringsend.

Going to St. Patrick's Church just on the Dodder

Got midnight mass with sister and brother.

What a great mass on Christmas Eve

It was when Christmas toys we no longer received.

And even when midnight mass came to an end

We still went over the Bridge into Ringsend.

The CYMS a great place to join

For a game of snooker what a great time.

We started to grow and come out of our shell

CY had teams and dancing as well.

Though what a buzz it was in midweek

Heading over the Bridge from Penrose Street.

Then came the time for the final shot

The CY experience taught us a lot.

And even when snooker came to an end

We still went over the Bridge into Ringsend.

Many places in Raytown made their mark

But biggest of all was Ringsend Park.

To play for Cambridge and learn your trade

Was taking your game to the next grade.

For many people playing in the Park

Was the very first step where a dream could start.

God Bless St. Patrick's, Cambridge and the CY,

Three amazing places growing up as a boy.

And until my days come to an end

I will always go over the Bridge into Ringsend

In Ringsend by Madison Tucker

In Ringsend, by the river's flow,
Myself, My dreams began to grow,
My voice a song, my feet a dance,
A world of magic and romance.

My laughter filled the cobbled streets,
A melody of youthful beats,
I sang in squares, in parks, in halls,
My spirit bright, My voice enthrals.

The neighbours cheered me every day,
Their friendly smiles would light my way,
With every note and every twirl,
I'd hoped to be Ringsend's shining pearl.

From sunrise to the evening's glow,
My hard work set the town aglow,
I danced through lanes and by the docks,
My rhythm echoing the clocks.

The Spar cashiers and all pub folk,
Would pause to hear the words i spoke,
My songs would weave a tale so sweet,
Of Ringsend life, a perfect beat.

Opportunities began to bloom,
My voice dispelling any gloom,
Invitations from near and far,
I became a rising star.
But no matter where my path would bend,

My heart remained in dear Ringsend,
With every stage and every light,
I'd think of home, my heart's delight.

The friendly faces, warm and kind,
Were always in my heart and mind,
Their love and cheers my guiding star,
No matter how hard or tough or long or far.

In Ringsend, by the river's flow,
A girl with dreams continues to grow,
My song a gift, my dance a flight,
In Ringsend's heart, forever bright.

Ringsend on a Sunny Day by Ashling O'Connor

I wander through Ringsend to Sandymount's shore.
Where the waves crash and the seagulls roar.
The beach is wide, the sand is bright,
A perfect place to spend a summer's night.
I search for treasures, hidden with care,
Among the pebbles, shells, and seaweed there.
Ringsend is definitely a place of beauty, wild and free,
The red and white chimneys stand out proud for all to see.
A village of history,
I remember the Old Bottle House many moons ago,
Once a unique gem, for you and I to behold.
Its walls were made of stone,
Its windows, glass and steel,
A place where stories were told,
And secrets were revealed.

A distant sight, hand in hand.
Of my favourite place in all the land!
The sun sets low, the sky ablaze,
The chimneys' shadows dance and play,
The beach is quiet, save that sound,
Of waves and wind, all night around.

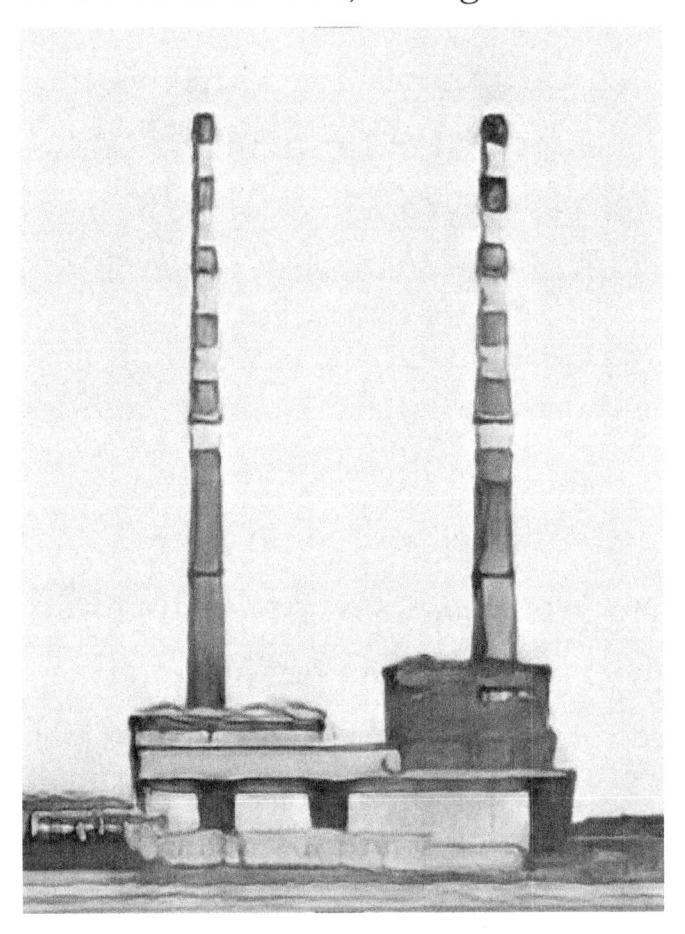

The Poolbeg Lighthouse by Thomas Gregg

Long walk out cannot truly describe
The beautiful scene before your eyes
Seagulls screeching overhead
Waves crash against granite walls
In the distance a vivid red speck
The Poolbeg lighthouse shimmers in the haze
Hardy half-moon swimmers swim like an attentive guard

As weatherworn fishermen stand to attention
And then it stands before you
History entwined with unanswered mystery
Its vibrant light saw so much pass by
Thick solid wall kept out storm and gale
Yes so, many ships sailed safely past
But others perished crashed up on rocks
Then you sit to forget, feel your heart's joyous beat

Sea spray soothes as waves collapse
Nothing matters here as life is at ease
The lighthouse watching out still.

On a Bench by Suann Moore

We watched as the Brent geese departed from the park.
We sat there until the sky went dark.
Holding hands,
Holding each other
In many ways.
I read our letters, all faded and torn.
They remind me of how the years have gone.
And I miss you, my love.
My dearest.
I clung to you in oh so many ways
Like a barnacle determined to stay.
As strong as those barnacles clung onto the rocks on the beach.
Hard, tough, unbreakable.
We reached.
Stood the test of time.
We will be here long after June is over

Long after the festivities.
When the tourists are gone.
It will still be you and I.
We are one.
You offering your coat when I'm cold.
Our stories will forever be told.
Echoes of us sitting on our bench.
People may hear our laughter years from now,
and wonder why they feel uplifted for a few moments
Sitting where we had so much fun.
Our giggles will leave an imprint in time.
That walk, our talk.
The afterwards we knew we had brought.
Making history, who would have though?
My Darling, how many words start with the letter F?
I recall those evenings with fond memories.
In Ringsend Park.

The Grief Manual by Sophie Gregg

Grief is supposed to come in waves they say,

But what if it never comes at all

I feel like since it happened

My body feels numb, and my mind feels raw.

But no grief I haven't sat up during a sleepless night

With water rolling from my eyes haven't encountered my fight or flight

Cause you know they say that will arise with grief.

I feel wrong for not feeling the way I imagined it to feel,

I feel like I am betraying her for not being sad,

But this forces me to believe it's not real,

Grief is not universal.

It's not something everybody gets It's not like the flu.

I believe I grieved while she was here

She was still breathing yet I had started grieving

I was grieving right up until she took her last breath

And then it stopped

It was like when the clock strikes 12,

The way you felt yesterday is not what you'll feel like today

It's different I can't force myself to cry

I can't force myself to feel what

society says you should feel when somebody dies

I can't I can't lie to myself

I can't feel the way society wants me to feel.

I'm stuck between

In the space between fact and fiction in the grey area

Is there a manual on grief?

Please just tell me how to feel

Because I know I miss you,

I know my heart breaks for you

I know my body aches for you

I know my eyes stay wake for you But I am numb

I am walking across this tightrope

And I am afraid that if I stumble just once,

I will fall,

I will fall into a state I've never experienced,

Grief

But then again, grief is not universal

But if it is and I don't like it can I get a reversal?

Another September by Eithne Cavanagh

…this one offers up a crucible of still warm sun

Iodine on the sea air, wet sand, pebble crunch

and green slime at the tideline.

Warming myself on a wall of ochre

Dalkey stone I admire its ashlars edges,

and fancy that I hear

the miners' shout and heave

chipping through the seam of centuries.

My reverie is fractured by a banshee Gull

proclaiming ancestral calls

unchanged through all her generations.

Kids have one last paddle

or make just one more sandcastle,

a Poodle dips his elegant paw.

I pocket the day in one seashell

encrusted with tiny fossils and am humbled

to hold a former life - calcified – since when?

Sunday Morning Walks After Mass

by Mick Brady

We used to take a walk, just you and me
Where the two rivers and the canal run out to the sea
The city was always quiet on Sunday's way back then
A day of rest for the working men

Across the bridge and down the steps
Weeds in the dried-up grass, boats and old fishing nets
Jinny-Joes blowing across the black dirt track
Flowers growing wild out through every crack

My small hand in your old leather glove,

It looked cracked and worn, but it felt like love

I still remember how it felt after all this time

How proud I was to hold your hand in mine

The canal would shine and sparkle as it tumbled out through the locks

Cranes on tracks through the cobble stones down along the docks

We'd cross the river on the ferry, then we'd come straight back

This was our own little world

After you'd gone, your coat hung in the hall

She kept it there and I'd see it every time I called

I still see it in my mind and it takes me back

To our Sunday morning walks after mass

The factories, coal boats on the quays

The Broken Wall, wheat lorries on the streets

The gas works, the dog track and the mills

The Bottle House, the Iron Bridge

The rivers still run and the tides still ebb and flow

But the ships are gone, factories all shut down

Sometimes I walk those street but now I walk alone

It's not the same, it doesn't feel like home

Everything changes but not some things inside

Like memories of you that I keep alive

Sometimes the mirror takes me by surprise

And I think it's you, looking through my eyes

Maybe someday someone will think of me

And remember the way I used to be

Some small hand in some old leather glove

That looks rough and worn, but feels like love

The Lady Re-Purposer by Eithne Cavanagh

bobble hats and single gloves

berets, baseball caps, one lonely mitten

bedeck the seaside path she walks

a kind person neatly speared a kiddie's

Mickey-Mouse-face-hat on to a railing

on Ringsend Road

a cardigan, blue, with silver buttons

a crocheted scrunchie of dayglow pink,

one shoe, she hopes its owner hadn't far to go,

she sometimes thinks about bringing

these lost things home to wash

and wind-dry in a fresh salt breeze

then she would lay the bobble hats,

that long red sweater where she found them

or where someone might, just might

recognise, or take a fancy to

a Fair Isle beanie, a purple mitt

or scarf to brave wild blowing spray

on second thoughts she decides

to repurpose knitted things, unravel wool

and reknit something multi-hued and wonderful

like cardigans of many colours,

or a patchwork woollen quilt,

shelter from a world of fearful drummings.

Blessed by Mick Gregg

Having a love for where you grow up
It can bloom your perception of the way the hound was a pup.
Is it memory or perhaps fact that puts these thoughts in my mind
Or is it the old familiar longing to be around my own kind.
The trials and tribulations of learning those lessons
Those painful experiences and joyful expressions
"It will make you a man, it will put hair on your chest
Putting your back into that oar or playing ball against the best"
These words drove us on - we kept trying
Teaching us lessons while prevented us from crying.
We tried to fit in, try to be as they are,

Whatever they do - we were close behind, not too far
Pushing forward when you are held back
Giving as much as you get
Looking out for yourself- breaking out of the pack.
Local phrases and the odd profound quote
helping us climb up out of the steep moat yet,
as I look on fondly from a far off place
I think of those worn streets and warm community

I feel blessed by their embrace
I recognize these words and thoughts were the spine that spawned some complexity.
It was the best place to experience the lessons
It was my streets, my park, my river, my strand, my neighbours and friends that blessed me with any form of expressions.

The RIC by Tim Flood

Growing up in the R.I.C.

A place I still call home

Though I left in 1986

To Canada, flew across the foam

Playing football on the road

Even though we had the park

Driving some neighbour's crazy

From morning until dark

Windows sometimes broken

Colourful language often spoken

Collections had to be made

But on and on we played

Adventures on the tip-head

By the bottler, and on the strand

Imaginations running wild

And the stories they were grand

Rowing on the river

Swimming in the Lochs

Scutting on the Lorries

And boxing of the fox

Midnight mass on Christmas Eve

Singing with the Choir

Cathal Fleming conducting

While we sang for a power, higher

Lots of Families struggled

As there were many mouths to feed

But people helped each other

So, everyone could succeed

The men they worked in Boland's Mills

The I.G.B, and on the Docks

While mothers worked small miracles

Keeping homes and cupboards stocked

Sally sold the papers

Dan Dunne, he sold fresh fish

Clyne brothers for your beef and lamb

Canton house, for your Asian dish.

And if you are very lucky

In the days after you've passed

The locals will carry you over the bridge

And your wake will be a blast.

The Republicans by Tom Flood

Oh lord I know you hear me

As I sit here in my cell

Tomorrow they will take my life

Please give me the courage to die well

Myself and my 3 comrades

Were found guilty by our own

For we wanted a united Ireland

Not leave six counties to stand alone

Oh, dear mother as I write this

Please don't worry or shed tears

Though tomorrow I must leave you

After only 18 years

We fought for a united Ireland

And if our lives must be the price

I would pay it ten times over

Wouldn't need to think about it twice

There is much that I am proud of

And regrets there are some too

I will have no wife to call my own

Or children to bring to you

But mother dear my biggest regret is

I will not see you before I leave

A chance to give you one last hug

As I know you'll surely grieve

the so-called leaders on this Island

seems have gone and made a deal

to give away six counties

it's not just sad, it sounds unreal

for those who fought for freedom

for eight hundred years or more

must be turning in their graves right now

wondering what did we die for

Republican is what they call us

Republicans we will die

For Ireland it has 32 counties

On this there can be no lie

United is how it started

United is all we'll take

For Ireland is our country

Not to be divided up like cake

Alphabet Soup by Thomas Gregg

ABCDEFG
HIJKLMNOP
QRSTUV
WXY and Z
Now I know my ABC's
Next time won't you sing with me

ANNIHILATION of children and women
BARBARIC cruelty by men once again
CROCODILE tears shed by politicians in power
DESPERATE people promised help but when
EARTH is imploding and slowly dying
FRIGHTENED grandparents nightly crying
GENOCIDE Oh god - can this be your plan
HELP me to understand as I'm a lone man
INJUSTICE done daily never ever addressed
JUSTICE from up high conveniently suppressed
KILLERS of millions remembered with statues

LOVE is it lost no as its always coming at you

MEMORIES repeated of such horrific days once more

NAZIS rampant as they kicked down your door

OH, why have we let this happen once again

PALESTINE war must be stopped now not when

QUIT with the continuous failure to say what must be said

RHETORIC used daily unfortunately just means more dead

STOP the one sided war irrespective of who caused it

TENS of thousands innocent dead please stop it

UNFORTUNATELY, too many people still look away

VENGEANCE has been let have its own way

WAR so one sided it's just continuous slaughter

XTERMINATION repeated this time on innocent sons and daughters

ZIONISM how can this be tolerated

The Widows' Bakery by Eithne Cavanagh

The buildings I designed penetrate the sky.

The blue I used to love now suffocates me.

Throwing off my cloth prison,

I move again with natural litheness

in the bakery where I knead and pat the dough.

The aroma of flat loaves cooling

spells a modicum of freedom, an unmeshed view.

Here, in the widows' bakery, the oven heat

rises with our mirth, a few hours friendship.

Sometimes at night I watch the crescent moon.

I cannot paint my nails, play music,

wear high heels.

I who created skyscrapers, hotels,

must now move silent, invisible,

(better were I illiterate).

Blinded by cloth, her tormentors a blur,

my friend was beaten for a ripple of laughter.

My small son cannot fly his kite to see

its multicoloured tails stream heavenward.

I smuggle my daughters to a secret school,

still safe ... today

What tools will they use to architect their lives?

My buildings will endure beyond oppression,

vibrant with music, kites and moondust,

nor crumble like the rations

I bring home beneath my burka.

Growing Up By Anonymous

Growing up in Ringsend, by the sea,

Where seagulls soar and boats roam free,

In the shadow of the Poolbeg Chimneys tall,

A place where memories rise and fall.

Strolling by the Liffey's gentle flow,

Past the docklands, where stories grow,

In Ringsend's embrace, the heart finds peace,

Where the city's hustle and bustle cease.

Children's laughter fills the air,

Playing in the Park without a care,

The smell of salt and seaweed near,

In Ringsend, where time is dear.

Growing up in Ringsend, a gem so bright,

Where the sun dances on the water's light,

In each street and corner, history weaves,

A place where the soul believes.

By Anonymous

Growing up in Ringsend is a blast,
The Community's kindness will forever last.
From friendly neighbours to helping hands,
Lifelong friendships in Ringsend expand.

In this close-knot place, we all belong,
Festivals and memories strong.
Local shops, bustling streets so grand,
Ringsend's care and love always at hand.

Cheers to Ringsend, where love never ends.
Childhood adventures, lifelong friends.
A special place in our hearts it will be,
Ringsend, forever cherished, you see.

Today by Eithne Cavanagh

… a blue silk gauze

covers Dublin Bay as far as Howth

a white ferry plies its course.

The Poolbeg chimneys needle skyward

as if some unseen gigantic darner

could mend a corner of this world.

Nearby, an Oystercatcher dips carroty beak

in search of lunch. Her piping call invites

surrender of thoughts that slither through my head,

Yet knee deep in water crisp and saline,

I marvel at how shivers of weak sunlight

tattoo snakeskin patterns on underwater sand,

And ripple-edges massage my aching feet.

If there is a god up there at all

… today I could believe.

Cure for a Whitlow 1958 by Mary Guckian

Facing my typing exams in the Tech,
suffering with a Whitlow on one finger,
I was very worried when a student from
the Drumshanbo bus that brought
students from around the area to the
school in Carrick-on-Shannon told me
a woman outside the town helped
people with ailments, making cures from
natures flourishing growth with herbs.

I cycled the eight miles to Drumshanbo,
finding the house on the hilly road with
tall trees, recalling a happy entrance
and meeting a lady who gave me a
little tin box, the size of the shoe
polish ones we knew, packed with
mashed up leaves looking like ointment.

Applying this to my finger, covering with a bandage for the next few nights gave me great comfort, the pain slowly leaving and healing. Passing exams I got work with Sligo County Council. After eight years I needed a change, travelling to many countries, working in a variety of jobs and for many different people.

Enjoying mostly a healthy working life I have never stopped writing and typing, thanks due to that wonderful lady helping cure my finger long ago.

THANK YOU FOR READING AND SUPPORTING

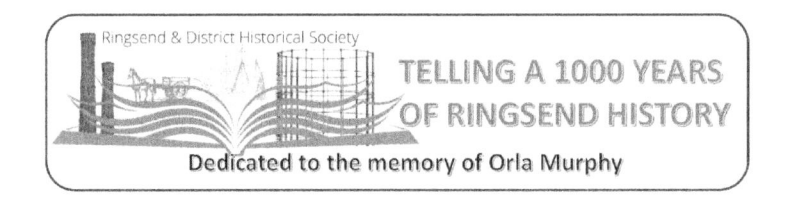

Ringsend & District Historical Society
TELLING A 1000 YEARS OF RINGSEND HISTORY
Dedicated to the memory of Orla Murphy

IF YOU WOULD LIKE TO PARTICIPATE IN NEXT YEARS BLOOMSDAY COMPETITION OR BECOME INVOLVED IN THE HISTORICAL SOCIETY CONTACT:

ringsenddistricthistorical@gmail.com

Printed in Great Britain
by Amazon